CSU Poetry Series XXX

Sarah Provost

INLAND, THINKING OF WAVES

Cleveland State University Poetry Center

ACKNOWLEDGMENTS

Grateful acknowledgment is made to the following publications, in which some of these poems have appeared:

AMERICAN POETRY REVIEW: "The Frog Prince"

BUFFALO SPREE: "Frostflower"

COLORADO QUARTERLY: "Scrimshaw"

DAIMON: "Naked Is the Best Disguise"

DAVIDSON MISCELLANY: "From the Stable," "Orphans," "After Rihaku"

HOLLINS CRITIC: "The Angel in Front of the Fountain," "The Orphans Construct"

MASSACHUSETTS REVIEW: "Shirley, Good Mrs. Murphy," "Obie"

MICHIGAN QUARTERLY REVIEW: "The Namer." MICHIGAN QUARTERLY REVIEW, Volume XXII, Fall 1983, No. 4.

NEW ORLEANS REVIEW: "Rumor"

POETRY: "Mercurochrome," "The Lonely Man Plans a Picnic," "Sometimes a Woman Wants a Love Without Landscapes," "Pastoral"

POETRY NOW: "Loup-Garou"

PRAIRIE SCHOONER: "Why Standing Still Was a Lot Like Walking, Walking Like Letting Go." Reprinted from PRAIRIE SCHOONER, by permission of University of Nebraska Press. Copyright 1983 University of Nebraska Press.

SOUTHERN POETRY REVIEW: "As If I Knew"

VIRGINIA QUARTERLY REVIEW: "An Incompleteness," "Inland, Thinking of Waves," "The Three Bears," "I Didn't Mean To"

I would like to express my appreciation to the Corporation of Yaddo and the Virginia Center for the Creative Arts for their support. —S. P.

Funded Through
Ohio Arts Council

727 East Main Street
Columbus, Ohio 43205-1796
(614) 466-2613

For Doris Provost and Edwina Trentham

CONTENTS

MERCUROCHROME

WHY STANDING STILL WAS A LOT LIKE WALKING, WALKING LIKE LETTING GO

AS IF I KNEW

i. You keep asking
how's the weather out there?
as if I knew. It's flat,
rectilinear. Wheat fields and farms.
I'm caught in the town, where Kansans
barber their shrubs to gumdrops,
and as far as I've walked,
I haven't seen one real flower.
This is not what you want me to say. I try
to believe in instinct, that the path
cut by a terrible wind
will guide itself while you search
all night for the good sleep.

ii. Room to room you rage
through the maze we made of our mistakes.
If I could recall
a balancing touch to give you,
the right smile, getting it wrong
again. I'd like to think
no instinct is deceptive
but black stones hang
from our backyard apple tree.
While you tally sad lambs, ignorant
distance has come for me, and what have I
taken away? Errant hands,
our domestic breath.

iii. You trace my footsteps in blue
carpet, while I climb to the roof
of the highest building in Hutchinson, Kansas
(which isn't much), watch lightning

ring the plains. Roads here
run straight and true, each decision a clear
right angle. You never knew
how often I left the house
to drive all night, fast, taking any hard turn,
hoping to lose myself. At dawn I glided
quiet up the driveway, tossed my keys
on the cluttered table, went in to watch you sleep
as the gray light grew stronger.

iv. What path? you ask, as if I knew.
Sometimes I'm a panicky animal, lost
in a field where the only sound
is the wind and you, calling me home
to safety in the burning barn.

SIMPLE

The white wave of the apple tree breaks
across the back yard. Somewhere
there's a small room
where I could bring flowers,

wild and blown, to adorn a plain table
and try to remember obedient sorrow
that comes and goes like the second hand,
the road home. Here, when the hard

knots of appleblossom threaten
to open, I close my eyes, thinking of first
light, something that simple. But your
particular name prowls the yard

from shadow to sun and back again. I glance
occasionally, but mustn't speak:
my voice might break
the pane. If we could transplant the rain,

crack the complex
code of light that says *bloom*,
it wouldn't change
anything: change has already

gathered itself and leapt.
In that room I could keep a primitive
balance, walk the unruffled ceremonies
of dusk. Here the wind stirs

white blossoms to an ocean,
a hundred tiltings. I wait for the wind
to rest itself, your name to spell itself,
the first slant of light to find the door.

WHY STANDING STILL WAS A LOT LIKE
WALKING, WALKING LIKE LETTING GO

You wanted straightened weather at the window,
magistrates, a country of white houses.
The very song of occupations.
I wanted allegory
out on the highway. The impossibly thin
rain invented guests and I
wanted a folklore like theirs, rabbits
running in the cattails
because the day was holy and dying of birds.

The guests demanded nothing, but I thought you
a motor above me. I wanted to distinguish
speech from singing along sexual avenues: anybody
can do it for mother. I wanted you
to be Iron Henry and burst your bands.

Daylight dwindled to
one out of ten. I kept waking up
smaller, wanting everything
but that body lying beside me with your hands.

FROM THE HARD GARDEN

Walking with open coats
in a false spring,
we walk toward winter.

It's to be expected,
that dark familiar
as the back of my lids,

pretending sleep,
and the cold no colder
than the last long summer

when our words hailed
on each other, cold buckshot
pocking our browned backs.

In our first garden
I was Eve and named
daylily, bellflower,

sweet grasses that grew
too high. You wielded the scythe
and named seasons. Now

nothing can keep the crocus.
from poking their noses,
tulips from shouldering

muscular torsoes too soon.
I want to lead them gently
back underground, into

their papery wraps. If I
lie down beside them
perhaps they'll sleep.

When we lie down in the dark
back to back
the small beads of bone

fit. Could we turn
this harp of December rain
back to the first

hard garden,
let the grasses sprout
to a second summer?

Then I'd lie down in
that grass, and you,
and name everything over.

THE AIRPLANE

I had been lost so long
even the wrong house
looked like home. Once in that door
I began holding silence, and the path
and the many dewed blades of grass
arranged themselves into deliberate
error and stayed put.

I should have refused
to sit safe as the best
china, locked away. But I said
nothing, and so lost everything
but the room for more hunger,
starving among friends.

The windows kept walking
one step ahead. Your touch shattered
my agreements with grief, lifted me
like an airplane, showed me what I
couldn't picture: the river

isn't asphalt, perhaps, nor the fields
stitched at the edge, but that scenery shouts
its facts at me:
I can't go back underground,
for even a short visit home.
The airplane blued

and cast me off
from silence, and from that hand, warm
and stupid with waking,
which touched me with nothing like
acceptance, touched only one cruel
and specific yes. Then slipped away,
in an instant away, like me,
so quickly gone.

RUMOR

I hear you've set out in a small boat,
stripped and greased in case you have to swim.
They say you passed the shoals two days ago;
I remember swimming in those shallows.

Here the yellow leaves are rattling.
Your son plays step-over in red boots.
I hear the clouds out there have hardened,
and you almost lost your bearing in the wind.

Here, the flowers hunker down into roots.
They say you've sighted land,
that your arms are burned brown,
that your hands lie thick on the oar.

All summer in his sandbox, your son
built beaches for your return.

AFTER RIHAKU

On the third day of your absence,
I would wrap myself
in your cast shirt, still empty.

In the third week,
I would reach from sleep,
embrace a darker pocket in the night.

All through the third month
I would scuff yellow leaves,
watch the birds gone.

Seeing a face in many,
the third year without you,
I would run after: not you, no one.

AN INCOMPLETENESS

haunts the best loved,
half the true body
missing most of the time.
The way we walk
alone, moulding the air
before us, cradling each other
in our empty arms.

2.

How deeply can you search
a wound, and still call it healing?
Making love, we say. As if
we could take it in our hands
and craft it, lovingly, the way a potter
tastes the clay for salts, runs wet hands
along a rim. And isn't the beauty
most in the flaws, in the bend
of the bowl's resistance? Which is why
I want to understand your story,

3.

which is why I want you
to hear mine. Listen:
against the white wall, a spray
of small exotic lilies,
bought to fill the space where you
are not, casts a zen silhouette.
I couldn't have arranged them
like that. Do you see? How carefully
they cup their shadows? How quietly
they heal the air they pierce.

IN MARCH

Sister snow, my veined hand's
gone amazed. That last life
was stingy, wrapped

in old skins: mosses and
winter, darkness
and wood. This morning remembers

the ancient sigh, plough-wind
greening dry weeds.
All night clouds gnawed

to a gauzy edge, calm planets swam
past the glass. Now the grace of rain
clatters on stone, a demon lover

hauls the day to song: your hand
lights the crocus, wakes
thrushes in my blood. March

with its rodomontade
sends the sky haywire. Flushed as dawn
in the body rush, I'm

riding on light
unveiled: my mahogany profile
shudders into fern.

LIKE THE LIGHTHOUSE

I keep signalling *Here, here*
while she burns steady and far
to call you home. Love, you're still

half-loyal, wanting it all,
lighthouse and morning star. Here,
where salt roses blow and gulls

flute the air, we could unleash
the creatures of keys, let slip
the soft beast of fatigue.

This is the charity
of harbor: how the sea leans
against the part of me that trembles,

your wide hands buoy me,
hip and shoulderblade.
While lighthouse oscillations play

études on the shade,
a baroque O rolls through my
quicksilver bones. In gulls' beggar dawn

constellations fade. I watch you
set sail: the rudder hungers
in pursuit, slate wake

signals goodbye. The lighthouse waits
return of its moment, bright

and gone, bright and gone. Porcelain waves
about to break to shallows.

STARTING OVER

The heart is memory's
pantheon, a complete catalog

of torture stories keeping lust
pushed down: a 60-watt bulb

in an old hotel, rain for forty nights.
When random passion

floods my interior river,
the sky dims with old grief

and the body's history murmuring
It's hard, sex.

Too many skid marks, too much
shattered glass.

***

My adamantine heart
has kept the peace,

but at night I rise
from the bones of sleep,

rise from my body like
water wandering,

and the visible air hangs
on a broken hinge of silence.

The moment after waking
is incurably honest:

We are not healed
by solitude. All that we own

is what we give away, we are
what we surrender to.

It's a gradual startle,
opening like a flower.

***

I dreamed as I grew older
I'd wane into consolations.

But a woman knows, finally,
how to come home to her veins.

If we send our enchanted anthem
into the sky again,

I won't regret
the sirens, the rain-slick streets,

the blind search for bodies in the dark.
No evidence

can hold me when stars dissolve.
I'll pay what I owe to sorrow, only

let me lay my body down
to bloom, bathed in rain.

MIRRORS LOVE ME, I'M NEVER THE SAME

i. A good clown
doffs his wild heart
in silence. In silence we return
to the same wait,
voracious and boring as
desert skies, any miracle
with wine. Slaked in midstream,
empty quays turn into the wind,
wandering sailors scheme
to recapture domains. I impose
carnival: Harlequin's stripped bare
as a girl in love, thumping Walpurgisnacht
and farewell.

ii. Or let's find an eiderdown room above
some rotgut bar, alone in a crowd
where cigarettes pass in the dark
somber as drums. We could trill
the break of law, jostle and roll lascivious
and curiously quaint. We could lie
like skiffs, helpless in the ocean's
romance, all absence
dissolved in a delirium of fog.
We could caress
this tempest, cleave to the heart's
dice. The cries of dolphin
carry us through night.

iii. Good clown, we're a dubious troupe. Our kisses
dazzle, then comes the slow repose
into our twin solos.
While we languish in the tedium
of a tame heart's false song,
a sailor high on holy water
sings chanties to the deaf.

INLAND, THINKING OF WAVES

See how the surf
rears and recedes, spills

and slides. Waves
don't move forward, energy

rises and falls, like the waves
snapped into a rope

connecting two people who stand
some distance apart. It only seems

the earth slips back
into the sea's embrace. And your hands,

sliding the bell of my hips, could be
that white crest, scent

of salt. No words for this,
only your groan, centuries old,

and the primeval keen
I wind higher and higher,

as if such joy
were sorrow at its root.

Surfacing, scrimmed with salt, we rock back
into language, try the only words

we know: *Hush,* you say,
hush. And *It's all right* and

Yes. Through the open window
traffic roars like surf. We lie

hundreds of miles from shore,
floating in our wake.

DARK SILK

No one understands the mystery,
how it sneaks past the guards in our sleep
and clambers up the delicate pipes of our bodies.
We store what love we can while the night,

too, sneaks past the guards in our sleep
and leaves no footprint in the dust.
We store what love we can while the night
stalks, dressed like a king in dark silks

and leaves no footprint in the dust
where we traced our names.
Dressed like a king in dark silks
and dim moon, the shadow of a tree

where we traced our names
fell across the faces of our children,
dim moons in the shadow of a tree.
The night was long and cold, it

fell across the faces of our children,
and the dying moon barely touched the water.
"The night was long and cold,"
you told me over and over. It was a dream

and the dying moon barely touched the water.
Though you have touched my waking body
you told me over and over it was a dream.
The motion of waves carries you away.

Though you have touched my waking body
no one understands. The mystery,
the motion of waves carries you away
and clambers up the delicate pipes of our bodies.

WEEDS

In yarrow, in thistle, the small joy
of knowing what to do
made solid: chicory knows
where to go blue, and how. By the day
it grows more real, further away from us.

When the sun rises, we forget our beginnings
in concrete dreams, remember only
how we shut our eyes to each other
for the first time. Listen,
this tearing apart will
surely release us, the slow pull
recalls our birth in the tides.

***

You stay out all day, and won't tell me
what you've found, some buildings
where the dark plodders of winter
whisk everything under their coats.
Yet even the buildings are gilded and
gently persuasive. What we ignore
announces itself as we wake: we won't tell
our dreams before breakfast, for fear
they'll come true before night.

***

We have to learn again each night
to be generous with our bodies,
give them to sleep and trust
they'll be kind and return.

This is the body I
found today, the body I pieced back
together, like blue air
repairing after a storm. All night

the useful spirits fought
our battles for us. They stuffed our dead
in the fireplace, trudged childhood
back to school, made

love to the stranger on the bus.
When night goes down, these angels
lay down their trumpets
and rest. Then we rise,

scavenge ourselves
along the beach where weeds
point after the wind
and dig their roots in deeper.

***

The weeds float past an insomniac,
for whom sleep is the little

death. We don't mention waking
over and over, so many small moments of

consciousness saying *Touch me.*
Do you remember the story that begins

with some man refusing some
woman, his reasons precise in his mind?

If they could lie down in a field,
they could let go gently

and come back to themselves: in their thin
tight skulls they have nowhere to turn.

The story begins
to end with that silence, neither appearing to know

that they both have bodies
or what they both have given and can keep. Long before

the story began, the weeds began, and the voices
of that man and that woman

went into someplace that was home
and would have stayed.

SCRIMSHAW

Daily, you dig deep under my skin,
burrowing toward the blind touch of bone.
Delicate with your jackknife,
you are the craftsman. You decorate
my ivory with quaint devices,
spidery calligraphy down my spine.

You string my ribs with serpents,
red and black. You rub in ink
for fine stripes. A ship sets sail
from my shoulderblade with a cargo
you won't tell. My hipbones harbor dragons,
the fourteen bones of my face
you trace with flame.

Commandments on my fingers, a disaster
down my back. You sketch your face
on each blank plate of my skull,
draw a blade along my breastbone,
and then, two hundred times,
you sign your name.

NAKED IS THE BEST DISGUISE

Because you have felt my basket of ribs
swell and heave under your hand,
you think you know what breathes,
what scrabbles and knocks inside.

Because you have wandered my palm,
mapped the rapids in my wrist,
you think you can trace
the small blue streams to their source.

Because you have charted
the slope of my thighs, and praised
for a pearl each small white bone of my spine,
you think you know who I am.

But even as I give this
body to your hand, I have motives
I don't understand, and couldn't swear
the skin you touch is mine.

PASTORAL

HEY!

It seems to be spring, sweetie,
here in the heart of the green
proprieties. The thirsty wind is a rascal,
makes quick work of our splendid

coifs. April! Delirious bag ladies,
busboys, mommies and tarts
sing hey to the grass and the birdies.
There never were so many babies

as now when we stand on our manners.
They are cupids, grazing daisies,
crawling for baubles among these particular
trees. And Rover, lying in wait

under the shade of the billboards,
intends to rummage whoever passes
and frolic their bones among
the hungry flowers.

THE FROG PRINCE

The house of the Greeks has turned
to a factory of voices, no one voice
collecting the songs of the moon, handing down
the ceremonies. Parallel hymns cross and fragment,
stubborn as winter apples or
a '52 Ford. Any idiot in a pickup
is part of a dynasty, every marriage has one
naked princess and a swimmer full of charm.
Have you noticed that neither sex

nor poetry quite pulls the thorn
from the lion's heart, your teeth from the hand
that loves you? What's to do?
And which is more real, the fabled Medusa
or my petit-pointe millefleurs? I'll be damned
if I'll let the dead kingdom of sleep
tunnel into yet another day. There are too many dead
anyway, we can't keep count. My rowdy aunt's voice

grew small, telling her own elegy: the joke about
the cowboy and the crescent moon. You haven't
forgotten the moon? She shed a little light on the heart
of Baltimore. Her gapped and deceptive matins
have been collected and passed down through at least

my hands. Have you heard the one about the Frog Prince
and the lawnmower? Actually, the lawnmower
doesn't come into this at all, it's just
some kind of Cartesian mirror, or do I mean
artesian river? What's art, anyway, but a different
dreaming, a common testament divided
between stars and things, things like quilts or the
guest of coal that overstays within
till kind nature explicates a gem.

PASTORAL

We travel a path that keeps turning into outskirts,
never quite arrives. The landscape seems
a bit daffy, with its flocked shepherdesses
propped in a drizzle. I think I've taken a bad
turn.

◁ CARPE DIEM   BEWARE OF THE DOG ▷

I try, but newly lit windows
archive nothing particular. There's grass
and children bellowing, scavengers of something
farther off, but try as I may, the true-made knot
unbraids. When I mistook the farmer for
eponymous lamb,

mutability blossomed everywhere, acanthus
after a summer storm. The farmhouse
gives in to analogy, pasture to beach, pebbles melt
to a dull pavanne where the shepherdesses stroll
with their sodden sheep.

My buddy here loathes the sea, keeps yelling
"Sorry, buddy" in a routine rant. I need
fewer friends, a good alias: seamstress
in love with a snowman, a scholar studying away
the cyrillic hours, or go walking
in a hunchback's coat. Ah, shit, let's hit

this tavern, join the crowd of snails
riding on glass. I like this place, with its gimcrack
chandelier, a moody tremor in the ambience. It's not
where I meant to be, but that's part of
the comedy, like that bug in your lager.

I DIDN'T MEAN TO

unbalance the flowers on their stems:
their brute grace fisted me silly. Now
I'm sodden as Sunday. Greeks
couldn't speak of my feelings, I'm a zoo baby.

Oleo hour, the sunlight seemed
a little older. Trellises of coreopsis
emerged graceful from the garden in my lap,
naked and apathetic. Listen, I wasn't
a conscious composition, my legs arranged like sprays
in an artless bouquet. The lower ranges of love

talk no-hands, but for you every sailor in the fleet
has to rush the rigging, each wave
a cause for captains. I trust the asexual song
filling my mouth with another burgeoning . . .

It's an intricate
resistance, I tell you, one part blind innocence,
two parts barbarian terrain. While I explain,
the cyclamen lets fall its rosy wings, forced
blossoms drop their petals on the floor.

THE ART OF LOVE

What's gone is gone, but if we remember
everything we did and failed
to do, aren't we doing it

again? It's a serial
predicament, the perils
we lash ourselves to, and night

coming on fast. If you'll forgive
the mortgage, I'll stroke your
fine moustache. This time

you wear white and I'll
be foiled. What's past
is past. Here comes the train.

A flurry of new snow
litters the common,
scribbles a fresh story about

the same old anomie.
A few slow clouds stroll by,

which is all right by me:
when the cold sun goes veiled,
it takes away

the little slab of darkness
under everything, leaves only

this even gray
like the eyes of a judge.
Today I could condemn myself

for any crime but passion.
Give me one good reason for February

and I'll give you my hat
with its wax fruit, my
ghost-of-tangerine lipstick, my sarong.

Let me lie down with the groundhog until
the crazed puddles mend.

THE GROUND SEEMS SO FAR AWAY

It's the match of the century:
fidelity and ennui. If Halley's
comet dropped by every night, who would
notice? No big deal. No doubt
about it, I want to be loved, just not
all the time. I haven't really
thought this out, but I'm not coming back.

I never did get to see the goddamned comet
and now it's lost in the light.
When I said we shouldn't have to
look to the sky for event, I meant
something like what I mean when I say
I'm not coming back, but only

gradually. Do you think the comet
is a fiction? Big empty spaces so far away
make gravity and return seem unnatural.
Listen, it may come back, but not me.

SHIRLEY, GOOD MRS. MURPHY

follows me everywhere in a wool hat,
the crook of her finger, her dicey
eyes. She offers me soup in a full cup,
she gives me bananas from out of her bag
in front of everyone.

She brings me strays and empties my pockets
of lifted pens before I leave work.
She got me my job.

Though I walk down dark alleys to shake her
she fears no evil. I beg her
to leave me alone, but she
says I should come and live with her
for ever and ever, amen.

THE THREE BEARS

I just left them there holding their breath,
summer dripping from their honeyed
muzzles. The wild circles of their night eyes
became taillights and went on without me,
speeding my life backward, faster and faster. I'd rather

have followed that arc of light, but the world blackens
a bouquet of weddings held to the bride's waist,
talks back to love sunk low. Snow
presses its lips to a mirror,
passing breath from one shadow to the next.
I plan my nights with my face in my hands,
like a serious child making weather turn its back.

It's more than I counted on, love half dead, this long
hibernation. And here I am, driving on ice,
yelling promises into the night,
wanting to own some wings, some ship,
white sheets sailing small away.

THE DUCHESS'S NONDESCRIPT DAUGHTER CONFESSES A WHELP

Parents of good will have so many words:
I shrank from advice, quite naturally, held
a virgin doubtfulness
between my misconceived knees.
My mother told her decades
of disappointed parlors,
followed the saints' bells
through milkweed veiled for confirmation.

I was the one shuttered from daylight.
Not having seen, I sent the world
on without me, while Mother and I sat reading
in overstuffed rooms, a family for the homeless
to point to with their lives. Immaculate
and light as smoke, I felt already
expected underground.

But then I was suckered by wildflowers,
admittedly wildflowers. Out in the air, I found
the crumpled roots of the river, a small frenzy
running the length of its body. The image runs
together here: body to body, water to shore
shadow to light. When I cup my palms
to my ears, I hear two hearts; in humid
dark, small veins unfurl.

Everyone will be different in heaven,
Mother. Myself, I'll be pure as a needle,
a blue filament. But for now
my good angel's body's a violin: I have
the melody by heart.

THE ANGEL IN FRONT OF THE FOUNTAIN

hovers in a stone light. We are having our salad,
our ham on rye, ought to get
going, we have reports to write.
      The hair of the angel lifts
in the gritty air.

We crumple our napkins, have a last
smoke, about to push back our chairs. Slowly,
      the angel lifts his horn.

Some of us smile and nudge the one next
to say or
      about to say *look, some sort of mechanical*
to say *did you*
about to wonder if
      about to rub

our eyes. The angel in front of the fountain
rises and a blast of horns taxis horns   a horn!
      The angel
has gone back to work and we've
      been here a long time, our forks to our lips

SOMETIMES A WOMAN WANTS A LOVE WITHOUT LANDSCAPES

Leave the abandoned cabins
unrevisited: I'm sick of archetypal
romance! You're always parachuting
down from a distance, a magician amazed
by his last best trick.

Cast adrift
in a wide-screen sunset, you scuttle off
to write down your dilemma on winter
bark, a delicate paper. You lay it all out
like a sandbar.

O we would be children in the foyer,
safe on the checkered surface
of a perfect world. We would be wild as hares,
eyes rolling under a ringed
moon.

Listen, the new moon is just another mouth
getting loud.

Come simply, without
your valentines, your heart-shaped
postcards from the Poconos.

For God's sake
hold your tongue and let me love!

UNDER THE RUSTIC SUN

Man, this is living, where dawn
drags roosters along back roads and as
the sun rises, stretches them high and eager,
pissed at being awakened from dreams of pullets,
but triumphant none the less. Son,

if a multitude of evil mouths
have made you crawl under barriers,
opening fresh wounds in your scaly elbows,
if you been kicked out of foreign ports
and dragged uphill, well,

here you got this mountain. It could be worse.
In Hallelujah County, it's always five o'clock,
always Friday, and in Spring a Flexible Flyer
always blooms on some hill, the sky shrunk down
under its runners. Everywhere else it's

Monday morning, hoarding hunks of hard labor
under the porch. When thistles hold their spiked heads
erect in the meadow, it doesn't have a moral.
Hell, any hot fool
can scrape a quarrel off the sidewalk,

but it's quiet here where no neon hums. So let's go
bucolic, where small furry animals
displace concrete and gin rummy sits sedately
in your blunt future. No moon tonight, Petunia,
Porky's got an apple in his mouth.

LOUP-GAROU

He loses himself by pieces:
the edges—ears, nails, teeth—
jut and fang. The last thin gut
of reason burns confounded,
dissolves in the beast's
perfect lore. For a moment's panic
he stands displaced, upright
in a dark suddenly mapped.

He drops to a lope,
pads of his feet kindled
by dry leaves. His tongue
lolls as he runs, keen and feral,
the man-spirit forfeit.
Breaking the thicket,
he is washed in the lucid moon;
pauses, and lifting his head
lets howl.

Mornings, waking degraded
in the deep woods, he feels
that howl, how the straight line
of his throat arrowed it clean
to the sensible sky. It whines
in his cropped ears
all the way home, what he meant by it
lost as he stood.

THE ESCAPE

For an instant, the escape started
sniffing its own trail, running
cranial errands out of the past: there are still
places in my body where abandoned landscapes

keep gates. I insist on hanging
chandeliers in the badlands, damask
over the family album. I've fleeced myself into
this cozy chill, swaddled in a lambskin,

while the escape lopes
like tumbleweed across the wild
islands, then circles back
to hunker down in the yard

and watch me smoke
in an upstairs window of this continent
house, which holds everything I need
except my vagrant face.

THE LONELY MAN PLANS A PICNIC

He wears his invitation on his sleeve,
imagining the landscape
partly undressed, the sky entirely
nude. Remembers that orchard on the late show
where brandy sojourned in a basket:
poppies, plums, the blushing skin
of music. Clotted sweets, and swans half-
buried under tossed bread. Ah, lunchtime,
glands!

Festival morning dawns the color of brine.
By noon, the erected tent looms a maw.
He wanders drunk through arriving guests,
a man in an amethyst
panic: all his social graces
reduced to a primal quiver, like
what happens to the larynx on the dance floor.
The sky goes licorice, thunder lunges
over Queen Anne's lace. Already, parasols
and organdy skirts cut crosslots home.

In the pavilion the headwaiter waits
forever in tatters. A lattice of
melancholy guests, fossil tongues taking food
from strangers. A cruel waste of grapes,
he thinks, looking for an out. But Lover's
Leap's been blasted for the freeway.

OBIE

Look at them skinny yard dogs slink
when I tune my steel guitar. I lay back easy
in the old Ford's bed, serenade the kudzu. Meanwhile,

back at the future, the whole scene hangs
on your slippery name, a ghost
of the vacant billboard.

What logic dropped you hump-backed in a manger?
Smartass movieman, suicidal queen, say hello
to this pasta-pants fat dancer, who knows the secret

life of the juniper. *There's rhythm down*
my back, pawing with soft shoes. My brain
blows riffs like smoke rings. When the last dog's voice

goes home, you'll stalk
through the Sears & Roebuck shadows, a low-brim
high-pocket in a parrot shirt, off to Memphis to

become a singing bruise. You're going to carry that
cardboard suitcase loaded down with momma,
sell it to the city for solid gold.

MERCUROCHROME

SLOWLY, WE FORGET

the days I spent with you, alone,
as I am now. As I am now, you wouldn't believe
my quick changes of meaning,
changes of scene and memory as I sleep
apart from you and snow floats
out of a lowering sky.
We're still connected: have you forgotten
how we fell in together, not
by accident? Like the snow, we were too many
and never the same.

Have you found me
in my absence, do I sleep beside you
once in every night? Is there one unnoticed moment
toward morning when I go,
kissing you lightly as if we had all the time
we needed? The longer we fail
to reconcile, the deeper we sleep. Next time

we won't be lovers, we'll be dunes,
our house the wind and the hard sky. Then the stars
will be meaningless, random in their connections.
We'll be unchatteled and without pain. Then
there will be so few stories
we won't have to choose
one to hold us both. Your labor will be silence
and mine the dark.

THE NAMER

There are rooms that defy their walls,
that refuse to define a space, to be only
air and light. Geometry is not enough;
miters and cornices, mouldings and joists
do not satisfy these overweening rooms.
They want to take part in the dusk,
would willingly trade their furnishings for night's.

A room like that often slants by the ocean,
making no pretense to be home.
The woman who lives there feels crest and trough
under her feet, she floats on the room's
assumed waters. She knows she belongs to this
white room, its fictions a truth
it wants to tell her. She waits,

naming herself over and over, carefully, the names
handed down to her, the names she hands down.
The bodies she wraps in don't contain her:
they grow impatient and move on.
She waits in her white room to name the dead:

Puppet-Master. Heart-on-the-Mountain.
Saint Solitude; The Lingerer; The Loving
Stone. Over and over, her fingers throw their bones

as she sits in her white room, which does not wish
to be a room, but wants to partake of the tilted
ocean, the soft fuming of fog. And she does not wish
to be a namer, would willingly give back the high
intelligence of stars and find the names simply,
putting themselves back letter by letter, the way
she, in her power and sorrow, broke them down.

AMONG PINES

How easily we chide the lonely
boughs, the wind scuffling a screech owl. As if
mere wall would have comforted, hearts
next door. Tonight I see

the white flag of your breath among pines,
watch your small blue car go stone
in early snow, headlights darkening
as dawn comes on. That car's message

should have plumed white behind you,
making tracks. But you took it
for yourself, having respect
for the delicate snow's own mind,

its white privacy. Nothing and more nothing,
with all its variations. All night
your sister listened to your loyal
absence, watched the dark

driveway whiten while you sat, a woman sleeping
with the force of still water. By morning,
your windshield drew a veil, cold
and irreproachable.

ORPHANS

Like mushrooms, the orphans crop up
overnight. They nod and nod
their small bald heads.

We are no real orphans here,
those aristocrats of the chain link.
We are all orphans of indifference.
Who could lose a mother
save by neglect?

We have failed
to keep them, poor birds.
We forgot the magic word
and they flew off, bright
and delicate and singing.

Oh, we say it now.
We send it up from our cots at night
like frosty breath, small ghosts floating
over the iron rows.

All our tears too few
to salt them home.

THE ORPHANS CONSTRUCT

The orphans, the blonde ones,
are building a harp in the attic.
They will string it
with strands of their hair and sing
Kyrie Eleison. They believe
this will bring their mothers
bursting back
through the small high window.

The orphans are weaving
a ladder of hair, the brown-
haired ones. They will climb
hand over hand and jump
from the highest rung,
trying to fly after.

The black-haired orphans
wheel daily over the yard
searching for bits of trinket,
foil, pretty stones to tempt
their magpie mothers. They make
a nest of their hair,
curl in and wait.

The faces of orphans
wear shiny and blank with time.
The flat faces of orphans
swing open to show
a lock of their own hair
tied in twine.

FROM THE STABLE

We are alone here.
While travelers snort and sleep inside,
tumbled on their pallets, I wait,
watch the moon set the frost blazing
on hay, on the flanks and breath
of heavy animals.

Wings, wings! My globed belly shudders
and it begins. Once I heard
billowing seas or wings
and a voice like the sea
roaring. This mindless tunnel
in dusty blankets, this grinding
was not announced.

What comes of this I can't remember.
I am dim with work.
My good husband sits bewildered
as I grunt and blur. He flinches
from my pallid sweat, my bulging.
I fill the chapel. He dwindles,
pressed small in a corner
by the weight of my event.

Burst through the dark
the born thing cries: a bloodrush
in my ears, like wings,
like singing.

THIS LIFE

One good slap from fate
and I could be back in 1948, my teenage mother
refusing her X on the paper.
Sleet on the windowscreen can't reach
this pool of lamplight, but my birth stretches
all the way here and beyond.
If she hadn't made her mark, would I
see this pine's chiaroscuro out my window?

***

I'm watching rain cling to the screen and freeze
in tiny squares. It makes a map of a city
I've never seen. If I live there, I have red hair
and work in a factory cutting glass. Evenings,
my mother and I play kings-in-the-corner and listen
for the whump of children leaving their beds.
They shuffle into the kitchen, rubbing their eyes in the
    light.
Under that lamp we slap red on black,
laugh and push back our chairs.
Just before sleep, the small drip of winter begins.

***

A door slams the past back together like bricks:
my son bursts in, demanding a sandwich. I'll sit
at the kitchen table while fog takes the pine,
binds me in my round tight dominion,
clinging to happenstance as if it were a vow.
I don't live in that city. It's that simple.

DIVERS

After her first shy voyage into
passion, a young woman is diving
deep into tropical waters. Back in the
dry world, her ruffled bed and stuffed
animals grow peaceful dust, quiet as weeds
growing under an elm. She never thinks of
her father under some tree, about to sleep,
gradually displacing the able-bodied
weather in a meadow. She never thinks of him
like that, hammock and beer, sleeping his way
away from her, flying toward the bottom.

She wants to go slow
in this ardent descent, floating down through
days. She thinks of her body, taking air,
her breasts blue in lagoon light; the way
water paraphrases the sky; her father's face
blue in an old photo, that young man's body
still lurking in the paunch.
She closes her eyes to the tame sky, end of day
bleeding away. She doesn't want to see
the sky calling her back, nor listen

to her father, his descent
in the same lagoon, and how at that depth
the sky looked the same to him, nonsensical.
He calls to her from below, a confusion
of noises that ridicule the body,
all the obsessions of a dying
animal. She doesn't want to lose
her father in that depth, but will not hear
of deepsea weeds, the palette of algae
on watery palaces only

a breath away. How quickly he sinks without
breasts to buoy him. She'd call him
back, but he would tell how
none of it was hers—soft flesh, silken
impulse, meadow nor lagoon—since
it was all his first. Now he's sinking
faster, toward narcosis, calling back
comments and admonishments. She doesn't want
to hear them, wants to sink slowly in her own

rapture. And he can't forbid her
if she will not speak. How can he
deny her if she won't confess
what's missing? His face floats blue
from below. Nothing's really gone so far.

FROSTFLOWER

Heart of the moon dividing:
two, four, sixty-four,
mulberry, thumbnail, eel-child, you.
You, unnamed, unknown,
the terrifying arithmetic cast wrong,
cast out of your weightless space
into another spin.

Frostflower, I remember
the terrible silence in the cold tin ear
while up and down the hall I heard
other hearts go marching,
hard boots in their mothers' bellies.

Week after week I spent lying
against gravity, listening with my body
for a motion, a message *I am*
that wouldn't come. Your red surrender
swelled to a flood and you were gone.
I began the slow curving back to alone.

On days like this,
when the sun is a frozen penny
and there is no sound but the moan
of old wood, I see you floating,
little mote, ephemera,
just out of reach.

MERCUROCHROME

I kneel at the brick border and cover bulbs
while leaves peel off the trees like Blue
Angels. It's a beginning,

like the first edge of bone
that clinked against your little spoon. *Look up,*
smile, flash. How you screamed,
while onlookers murmured *adorable* and mama
laughed, seeing the smile already under glass.

Tonight, early October dusk, small armies
surge and retreat in crabapple wars,
flesh packed on nervous armatures
with only slight variation. You run

everywhere, wrapped in your own familiar
wind, hear bells and whistles call
curfew from lighted doorways and never
come, preferring to hunker down with
your kind. Paths through vacant lots
seem to go on forever with no branching,

but suddenly branch. A flash of wrath:
the corps, in angry unison, peel off
and leave you alone in Sherwood.
When I bell you home, you come
without your shadow.

What can I give you for poultice? I could quote
What we depart from is not the way
or say how the cat followed after,
digging up bulbs to bat and rebury where

they'll bloom unexpected after snow.
But the alphabet itself is broken,
half each letter gone. I grow brisk,
move on. After all, mother knows

tomorrow will be different, and the same
deck shuffled and redealt in the four
familiar suits. Late, you murmur
down weirs of sleep: the crabapple tree
sucked into the ground, ocean
emptying under a swimmer, silhouettes
you can see stars through.

I used to paint red daisies
on your elbows, knees. Mercurochrome,
merthiolate, iodine, good night.

\